A Tree Grows in Brooklyn

Betty Smith

STUDENT PACKET

NOTE:

The trade book edition of the novel used to prepare this guide is found in the Novel Units catalog and on the Novel Units website. Using other editions may have varied page references.

Please note: We have assigned Interest Levels based on our knowledge of the themes and ideas of the books included in the Novel Units sets, however, please assess the appropriateness of this novel or trade book for the age level and maturity of your students prior to reading with them. You know your students best!

ISBN 978-1-58130-953-9

Copyright infringement is a violation of Federal Law.

© 2020 by Novel Units, Inc., St. Louis, MO. All rights reserved. No part of this publication may be reproduced, translated, stored in a retrieval system, or transmitted in any way or by any means (electronic, mechanical, photocopying, recording, or otherwise) without prior written permission from Novel Units, Inc.

Reproduction of any part of this publication for an entire school or for a school system, by for-profit institutions and tutoring centers, or for commercial sale is strictly prohibited.

Novel Units is a registered trademark of Conn Education.

Printed in the United States of America.

To order, contact your local school supply store, or:

Toll-Free Fax: 877.716.7272
Phone: 888.650.4224
3901 Union Blvd., Suite 155
St. Louis, MO 63115

sales@novelunits.com

novelunits.com

Name _____

A Tree Grows in Brooklyn
Activity #1 • Prereading
Use Before Reading

Directions: Complete the following chart. Write what you think are the causes and effects of poverty. Then write some possible solutions to the problem of poverty.

Causes
_____
_____
_____

Effects
_____
_____
_____

Poverty

Solutions
_____
_____
_____
_____
_____
_____
_____
_____

Name _____

A Tree Grows in Brooklyn
Activity #2 • Prereading
Use Before Reading

Getting the "Lay of the Land"

Directions: Prepare for reading by answering the following short-answer questions.

1. Who is the author?
   _____

2. What does the title suggest to you about the book?
   _____
   _____
   _____
   _____

3. When was the book first copyrighted?
   _____

4. How many pages are there in the book?
   _____

5. Thumb through the book. Read three pages—one from near the beginning, one from near the middle, and one from near the end. What predictions can you make about the book?
   _____
   _____
   _____
   _____

6. What does the cover suggest to you about the book?
   _____
   _____
   _____
   _____

Name _____

A Tree Grows in Brooklyn
Activity #3 • Vocabulary
Chapters 1–6, Pages 5–54

Vocabulary Chart

serene (5)	somber (5)	ragamuffins (7)	inveigled (10)
Messiah (12)	tenement (12)	*coup de grace* (29)	placidly (34)
consumption (39)	pulp magazine (43)	patriarch (45)	*goyem* (45)
genuflected (49)	aristocratic (53)		

Directions: Write each vocabulary word in the left-hand column of the chart. Complete the chart by placing a check mark in the column that best describes your familiarity with each word. Working with a partner, find and read the line where each word appears in the story. Find the meaning of each word in the dictionary. Together with your partner, choose ten of the words checked in the last column. On a separate sheet of paper, use each of those words in a sentence.

Vocabulary Word	I Can Define	I Have Seen/Heard	New Word For Me

Name _____

A Tree Grows in Brooklyn
Activity #4 • Vocabulary
Chapters 7–14, Pages 57–123

vacuous (58)	conscripted (61)	latent (62)	hoyden (64)
enigma (66)	beguiling (70)	Purgatory (72)	consternation (76)
caul (78)	surreptitiously (78)	commiserate (94)	paradoxically (96)
delirium tremens (98)	consummate (102)	impotence (110)	disdain (111)
lassitude (115)	temporized (121)		

Directions: Use the words from the vocabulary list to complete the following analogies. Select five of the remaining vocabulary words and create your own analogies for those words. Exchange your analogies with a partner and complete each other's.

1. FONDNESS is to DISLIKE as CALMNESS is to _____.

2. CONFIDENT is to SURE as FOOLISH is to _____.

3. ENERGY is to VIGOR as WEARINESS is to _____.

4. SECURED is to PROTECTED as DRAFTED is to _____.

5. REWARD is to HEAVEN as PURIFICATION is to _____.

6. ENVISIONING is to VISUALIZING as ENTICING is to _____.

7. LIFE is to DEATH as POWER is to _____.

8. IMPORTANT is to INSIGNIFICANT as ACTIVE is to _____.

9. ALLEGORY is to METAPHOR as PUZZLE is to _____.

Name _____

A Tree Grows in Brooklyn
Activity #5 • Vocabulary
Chapters 15–32, Pages 127–248

Crossword Puzzle

prodigiously (135)	languorously (135)	querulously (140)	scapegoat (152)
recalcitrant (152)	macabre (154)	subterfuge (154)	pariahs (160)
unorthodox (174)	disconsolately (182)	bawdy (193)	eulogized (204)
compunction (213)	bedlam (219)	plutocrats (219)	cryptically (225)
interlocutor (233)	prosaic (243)		

Directions: Select ten vocabulary words from above. Create a crossword puzzle answer key by filling in the grid below. Be sure to number the squares for each word. Blacken any spaces not used by the letters. Then, write clues to the crossword puzzle. Number the clues to match the numbers in the squares. The teacher will give each student a blank grid. Make a blank copy of your crossword puzzle for other students to answer. Exchange your clues with someone else and solve the blank puzzle s/he gives you. Check the completed puzzles with the answer keys.

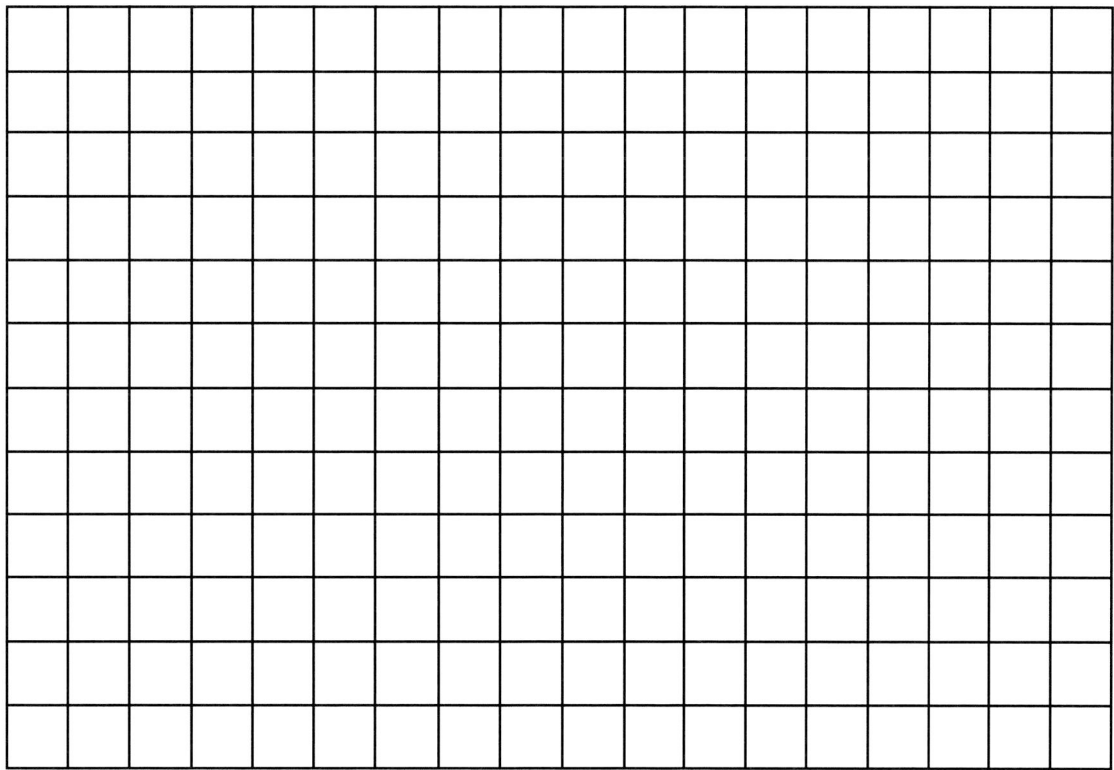

Name _____

A Tree Grows in Brooklyn
Activity #6 • Vocabulary
Chapters 33–42, Pages 249–360

Word Map

hypocrites (249)	corollary (272)	inscrutable (278)	plaintively (287)
fastidious (292)	inducements (305)	contemptuously (321)	reformatory (324)
abjectly (324)	diffused (339)	teamster (340)	mollified (342)
capitalists (348)			

Directions: Complete the word map for seven vocabulary words from the list above. Share your completed maps with the class.

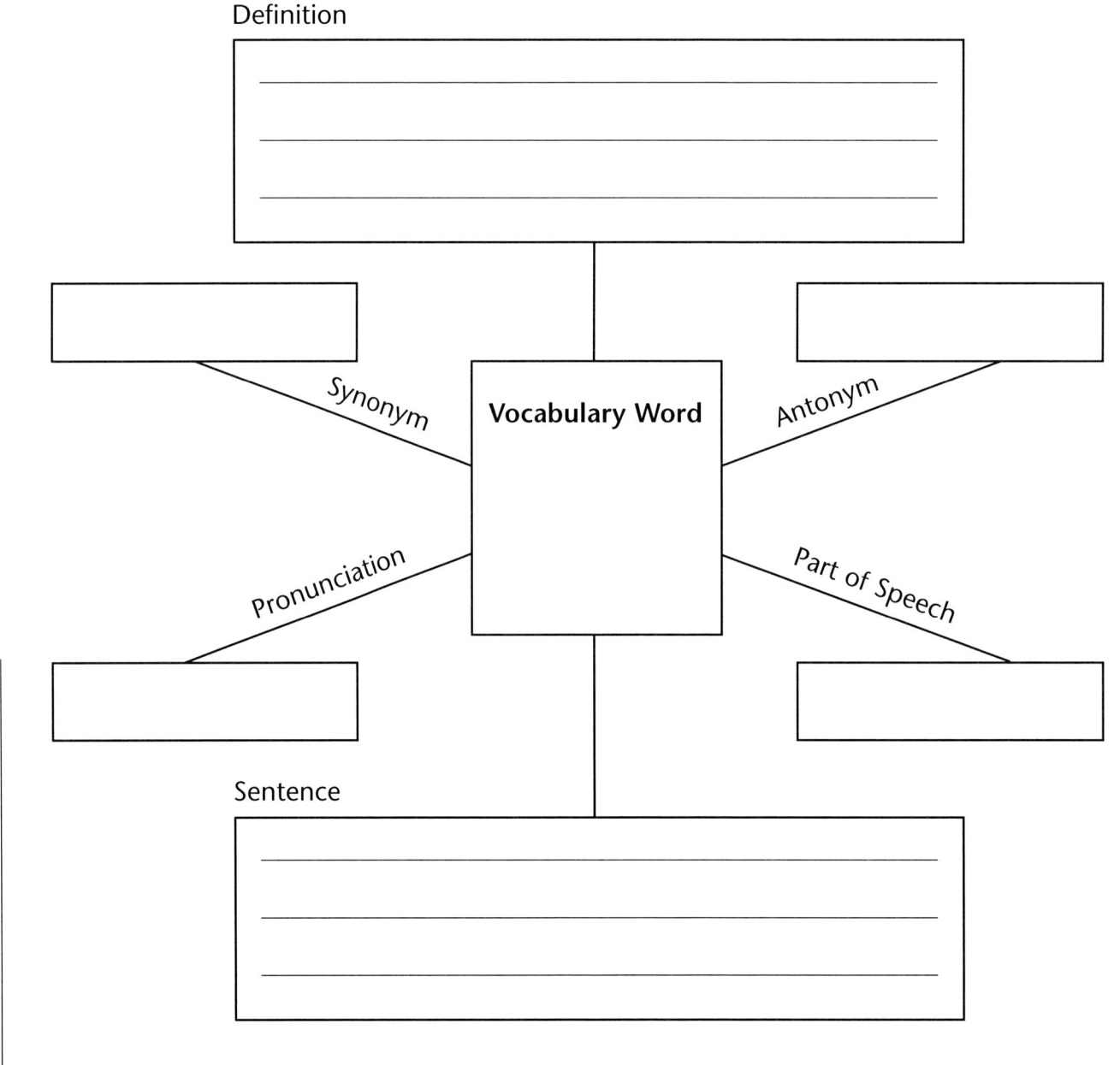

Name _____

A Tree Grows in Brooklyn
Activity #7 • Vocabulary
Chapters 43–56, Pages 363–493

Vocabulary Sentence Sets

cynically (364)	covertly (365)	ironical (366)	borough (372)
benignly (381)	spats (392)	cacophony (400)	parody (401)
magnanimously (406)	rhetorically (412)	dyspepsia (422)	matriculate (436)
luminous (468)	poignancy (476)	prohibition (485)	desultory (488)

Directions: Choose 15 vocabulary words from the list above. Write the words on the numbered lines below.

1. _____ 2. _____
3. _____ 4. _____
5. _____ 6. _____
7. _____ 8. _____
9. _____ 10. _____
11. _____ 12. _____
13. _____ 14. _____
15. _____

On a separate sheet of paper, use each of the following sets of words in an original sentence. Your sentences should show that you know the meanings of the vocabulary words as they are used in the story.

Sentence 1: words 8 and 4
Sentence 2: words 9 and 3
Sentence 3: words 1 and 10
Sentence 4: words 11 and 7
Sentence 5: words 15 and 13
Sentence 6: words 3 and 6
Sentence 7: words 12 and 4
Sentence 8: words 14 and 9
Sentence 9: words 5 and 2
Sentence 10: words 7 and 6

Name _____

A Tree Grows in Brooklyn
Study Guide

Directions: Answer the following questions on a separate sheet of paper. Use your answers in class discussions, for writing assignments, and to review for tests. Starred questions indicate thought or opinion questions.

Book One: Chapters 1–3, pp. 5–38

1. What is the setting of the novel?
2. Identify the protagonist and her brother and give two facts about each of them.
3. *What is the name of the tree in Francie's yard? Why do you think this tree is significant?
4. *How do Francie and Neeley spend their Saturdays? How do you think they feel about Carney and Cheap Charlie?
5. Identify Francie's parents and give two characteristics of each of them. What are their occupations?
6. *What is the ultimate ambition of the boys in Brooklyn? Why do you think this is important to them?
7. How does Francie feel about the library and the librarian? What is her reading plan?
8. Briefly explain Johnny's work habits and why the Union is important to him. Identify the song he always sings as he is coming up the stairs. How does Francie respond to him?
9. *What is Johnny's rationale for drinking? Do you believe this is the real reason he continues to drink? Why or why not?
10. *What does Johnny own that he would never pawn? Why do you think he refuses to part with them?

Book One: Chapters 4–6, pp. 39–54

1. Who are Flossie and Henny Gaddis? What is wrong with Henny? What three things does Flossie do each week?
2. *Why does Francie grow uneasy while looking at Flossie's costumes? Why do you think this is significant?
3. Briefly describe Sissy. How does Francie feel about her?
4. *Where does Francie go with Maudie Donavan? What do you think this incident reveals about Francie?
5. What must Francie and Neeley read each night?
6. *How does the Nolan family react to Johnny's arrival after work? What do you think this reveals about the relationship between Johnny and Katie? between Johnny and his children?
7. *Prediction: Will Johnny overcome his drinking problem?

Name _____

A Tree Grows in Brooklyn
Study Guide
page 2

Book Two: Chapters 7–10, pp. 57–97

1. Briefly explain how Johnny and Katie meet and initially react to each other.
2. Identify Katie's parents and give two adjectives that describe each of them.
3. *What does Mary Rommely request of her children's teacher? Why do you think she believes this will protect them from their father?
4. Who is Sissy's first husband? How old is she when she marries him? How many children do they have? What happens to them?
5. *How many times does Sissy marry by the time she is 24? How many children does she have? What happens to her children? How do you think this affects a woman?
6. Whom does Evy marry? How does she feel about her husband? What does she want for her children?
7. *To whom does the following statement refer: "they were made out of invisible steel"? What do you think this means?
8. How many sons does Ruthie Nolan have? What do they do for a living? What is their "destiny"?
9. What attributes does Francie inherit from her parents? How does she differ from each of them?
10. What does Johnny do the night Francie is born? How does her birth change Johnny's and Katie's lives?
11. State three things Mary Rommely suggests that Katie do after Francie's birth.
12. How does Neeley's birth affect Katie's relationships with Johnny and Francie?

Book Two: Chapters 11–14, pp. 98–123

1. How does Johnny celebrate his "voting" birthday? What is the effect of this celebration?
2. *How does Sissy help Johnny through this difficult time? What does she caution Katie not to do? Why do you think Katie agrees to comply?
3. What are Sissy's two great failings?
4. Why do the Nolans move away from Bogart Street? What effect does this move initially have on Johnny?
5. *How do the children in the neighborhood react to Francie? Why? What effect does this have on her? How would you feel if you were Francie?
6. With whom does Francie play while living on Lorimer Street? How does this affect her?
7. What two things does Sissy do that cause the Nolans to move from Lorimer Street? How do these incidents affect her relationship with Katie and the family?

Name _____

A Tree Grows in Brooklyn
Study Guide
page 3

8. Why must Francie wait a year before going to school?
9. *What does Johnny say about their third home? What do you think this implies?

Book Three: Chapters 15–24, pp. 127–189

1. *What does the girl in the schoolyard do when Francie tries to touch the blackboard erasers? Why do you think the girl does this? How does Francie react?
2. What does Francie think the airshaft looks like? Why?
3. How do the Nolans acquire a piano? From whom does Katie take piano lessons? How does she pay for them? How do Francie and Neeley learn to play?
4. How does the doctor treat Francie when she goes for her vaccinations? What effect does this have on Francie? Why is the nurse's reaction to Francie ironic?
5. *Briefly explain three of Francie's expectations of school and contrast them with the reality she experiences. Which of these do you think is the hardest for her to accept?
6. What happens to Francie that causes Sissy to confront the teacher? What is the result for Francie?
7. What does Katie do to protect her children from vermin and disease in school? What effect does this have on her children?
8. Briefly explain Francie's reaction to school and learning to read.
9. How does Johnny address Francie's desire to go to a different school? How does this "new" school differ from the "old" one?
10. How does Johnny feel about politics? How does he feel about women voting?
11. *What happens to Francie's tickets at the political picnic? Who gives her more? Why do you think this incident is significant?

Book Three: Chapters 25–32, pp. 190–248

1. What causes Johnny to drink more heavily? When Johnny sobers up after a period of heavy drinking, how does he behave?
2. Why does Francie tell her first "organized" lie? What are the results of this lie?
3. *How do Francie and Neeley get a Christmas tree? Explain why you do or do not think the tree man is fair to the children.
4. How does Katie feel about the children's acquisition of the tree? What does she decide about her children?

Name _____

A Tree Grows in Brooklyn
Study Guide
page 4

5. *Why does Francie tell another big lie? How would you feel if you were Francie? What does Francie learn about her name that eases her conscience?

6. *Identify three changes in Francie's life between her 11th and 12th birthdays. Which of these do you think impacts her the most?

7. Why does Johnny decide to take his children to the ocean? Who else goes with them? Identify three disastrous results of this adventure.

8. Why do the neighborhood women mistreat Joanna? What do they do to her? What causes them to leave her alone? What effect does this have on Francie?

9. *What do Francie's diary entries reveal about Johnny and the family's plight? What does the last entry say? How do you think this curiosity will affect her?

Book Three: Chapters 33–37, pp. 249–299

1. *What does Johnny do to protect his family from the neighborhood sexual predator? Do you think this is a wise decision? Why or why not?

2. Where does the predator attack Francie? What happens to him? How does Johnny help Francie overcome her terror?

3. *Where does Sissy plan to get a baby? How do the parents of the unwed mother-to-be treat their daughter? How do you think a similar situation would be handled in today's society?

4. What does Johnny think about the way Sissy gets the baby? What is Katie's rationale?

5. *What do you think Katie whispers to Johnny after they finish discussing Sissy's baby? How does Johnny change after this? Why do you think he is changing?

6. What happens at the Waiters' Union to make Johnny so distraught? What does he refuse to give the Waiters' Union?

7. What causes Johnny's death? What does Katie insist that the doctor list as "cause of death"? How much does his funeral cost?

8. What convinces Francie and Neeley to view their father in his coffin? How does Francie react?

9. What concrete objects of Johnny's remain?

10. What does Sissy's conversation with Katie after the funeral reveal about Katie?

11. How do Francie and Neeley cope with their father's death? How does Katie try to help them?

Name _____

A Tree Grows in Brooklyn
Study Guide
page 5

Book Three: Chapters 38–42, pp. 300–360

1. Why doesn't Francie want to return to school after the Christmas vacation? How does her mother react? What does Evy think Katie should do?

2. How does Mr. McGarrity feel about Johnny and his family? How does he help Katie and the children?

3. What does Francie conclude about Johnny after Mary Rommely's explanation of ghosts?

4. *How does Francie change her writing after Johnny's death? How does her teacher react to the change? What do you think Miss Garnder should have done?

5. *How does Francie react to Miss Garnder's calling her stories "sordid"? Why do you think she reacts this way? What does this incident cause Francie to do?

6. How does Francie help her mother at the time of the baby's birth? Why does Evy send her away?

7. What does Katie name the baby? Why does she choose this name?

8. What surprise does Francie receive at her graduation? How does this happen? How does she react?

9. What are Katie's thoughts about her children's education the night of their graduation?

10. How much does Katie tip the waiter after the graduation party? What is her rationale? How does Francie react?

11. *Prediction: Will Francie and Neeley go to high school?

Book Four: Chapters 43–46, pp. 363–407

1. What are Francie's and Neeley's first jobs after graduation? How do the other girls treat Francie at first? What makes them change?

2. *What do Francie and Neeley do with their first week's pay? How does Katie react? Why?

3. For how long does Francie work before the layoff? What is her next job?

4. What promotion does the boss offer Francie? How does she initially respond?

5. What does Katie decide about Francie's and Neeley's continuing education? How do they react? How does Katie explain her decision?

6. *Why does Francie think she and Katie conflict so often? To what does Francie compare her family? Do you agree with this analogy? Why or why not?

7. Identify two positive changes in the Nolan family a year after Johnny's death. How have Francie's feelings about his death changed?

Name _____

A Tree Grows in Brooklyn
Study Guide
page 6

8. *What type of Christmas tree do Francie and Neeley buy? What do they name the tree? What do you think the tree symbolizes?

9. *What happens as the Nolans and their neighbors sing "Auld Lang Syne" on New Year's Eve? Why do you think this is significant?

10. *Why does Katie add liquor to Francie's and Neeley's drinks on New Year's Eve? How do they react to the liquor? What do you think this indicates?

Book Four: Chapters 47–54, pp. 408–472

1. What news does Sissy receive about her first husband? How does she react?

2. What does Steve discover about Sissy's second husband? What do he and Sissy do after learning this information?

3. *Who told Sissy about Little Sissy's birth mother? What do you think Sissy's revelations about the baby and her birth mother imply?

4. *What is the newspaper headline on April 6, 1917? What does Francie put in her "Time Capsule" on this date? Why do you think she chooses these items?

5. *Why does Francie lose her job at the Model Press Clipping Bureau? Do you think she'll ever receive the education she wants? Why or why not?

6. What type of work does Francie do at her new job? How does her work schedule benefit her educationally?

7. *Who is Ben Blake? How does he help Francie? What is their relationship after the college semester ends? What do you predict for their future?

8. What does Sissy plan to do when her baby is born that no one in her family has ever done? How do her mother and sisters react? What is the result of her decision?

9. How does Francie meet Lee Rhynor? How does she feel about him?

10. What does Lee ask Francie to do the night before he is scheduled to leave? How does she respond? What does he ask her to promise him?

11. *What does Francie discover about Lee after he leaves? How? How does she react? Why do you think he allowed her to believe he loved her?

12. *How does Katie react when Francie tells her about Lee? What do you think this reveals about Katie?

13. How does Katie respond to McShane's proposal of marriage? What does he want to do concerning her children?

Name _____

A Tree Grows in Brooklyn
Study Guide
page 7

Book Five: Chapters 55–56, pp. 475–493

1. Where does Francie plan to go to college? Who chooses this college for her?
2. Give three characteristics of Ben Blake. What does he give Francie? Why? How does Francie feel about him?
3. How much money does McShane give Katie as a wedding present? What does she do with $200.00 of this money? Why?
4. Trace Francie's steps as she walks through her neighborhood for the last time.
5. *Identify three things Francie packs to take with her. What about each of these items is important to her?
6. What does Francie do for Neeley just before he leaves for the show? What does he do that reminds her of Johnny?
7. *Identify the last two things Francie observes before she leaves. What do you think these symbolize to her?

Name _____

A Tree Grows in Brooklyn
Activity #8 • Comprehension
Use During and After Reading

Fishbone Map

Directions: Consider the causes that led to the effect given. List cause 1, 2, 3, 4 (as appropriate). Add details to support the causes you list.

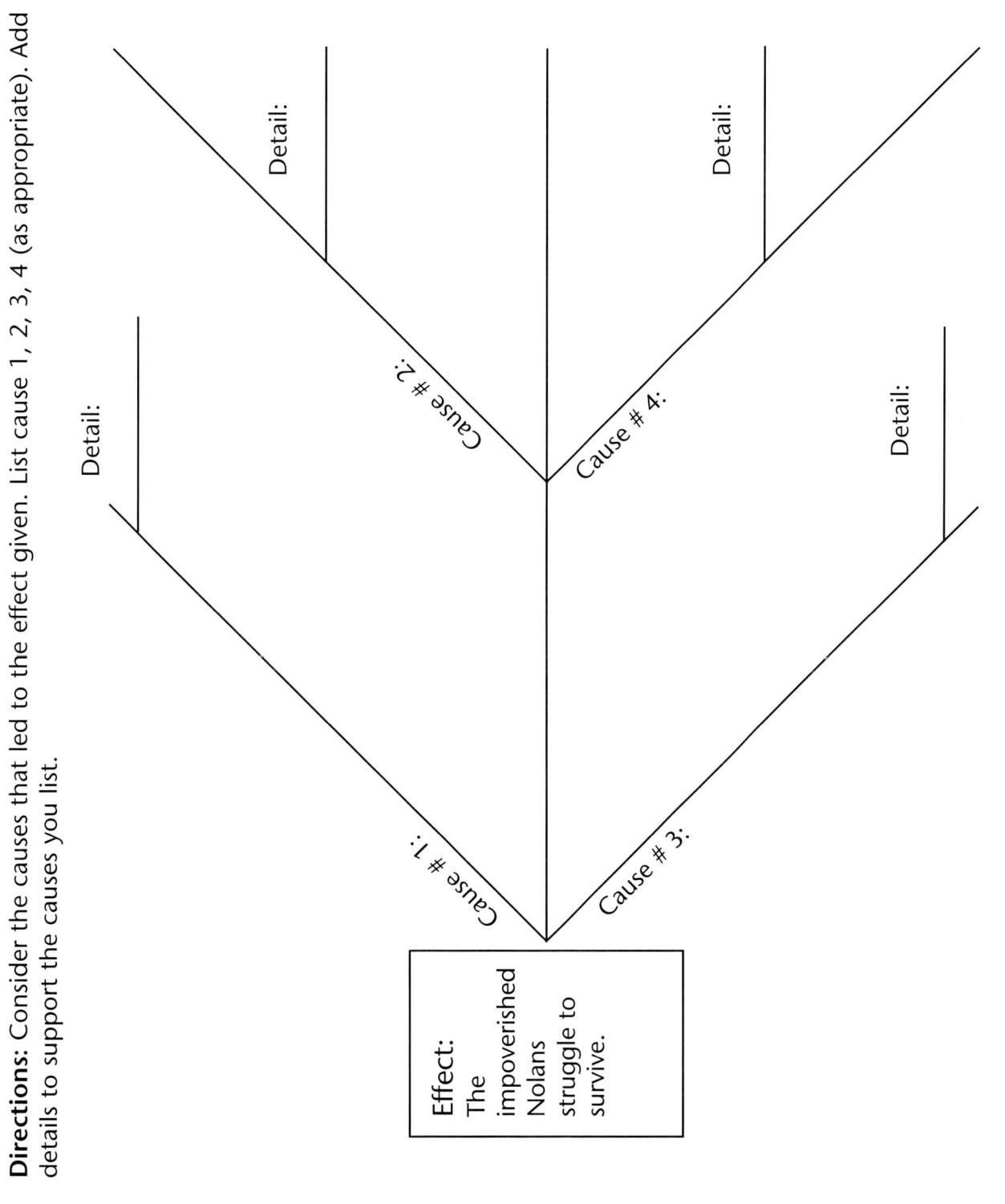

Name _____

A Tree Grows in Brooklyn
Activity #9 • Character Analysis
Use During and After Reading

Character Analysis

Directions: Label the boxes below with the names of characters who appear in the novel. Working in small groups, discuss the attributes of the various characters. In each character's box, write several words or phrases that describe him or her.

Name _____

A Tree Grows in Brooklyn
Activity #10 • Character Analysis
Use During and After Reading

Feelings

Directions: Complete the chart below for Francie Nolan.

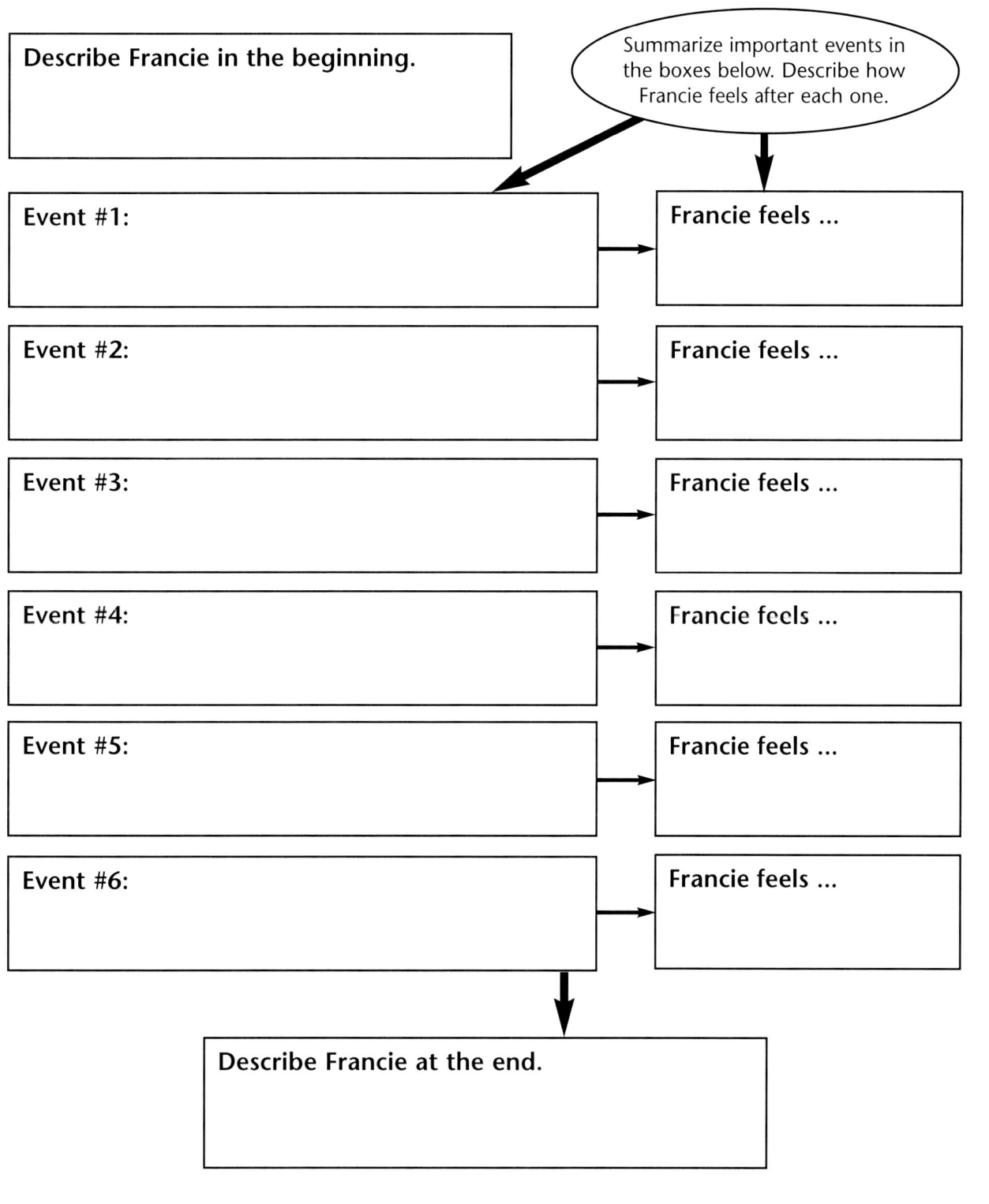

Name _____

A Tree Grows in Brooklyn
Activity #11 • Comprehension
Use During and After Reading

Sociogram

Directions: A sociogram shows the relationship between characters in a story. Complete the sociogram below by writing a word or phrase to describe the relationships between the characters. Remember, relationships go both ways, so each line requires a descriptive word.

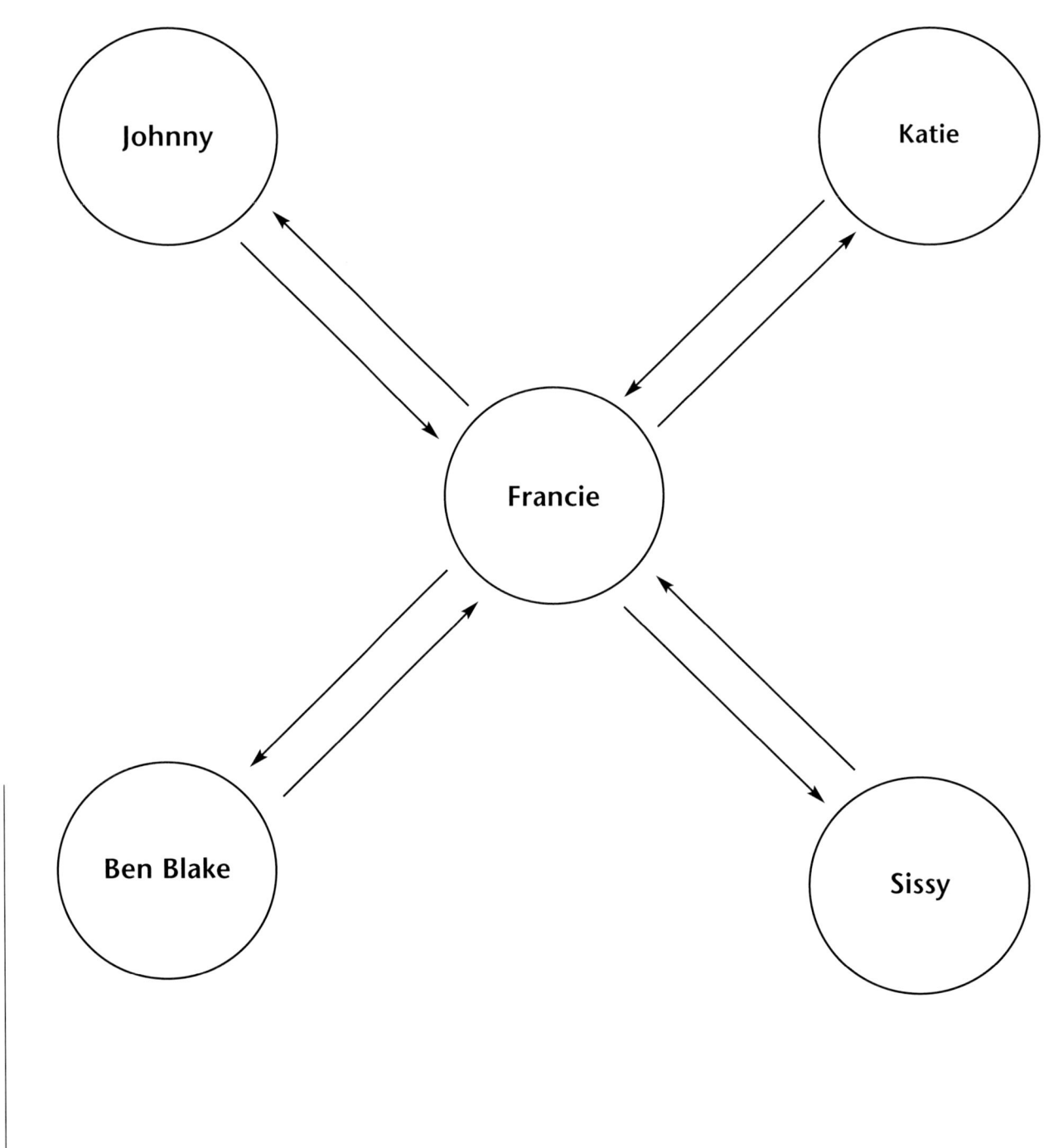

Name _____

A Tree Grows in Brooklyn
Activity #12 • Character Analysis
Use During and After Reading

Characters With Character

Directions: A person's **character** is evaluated by his or her actions, statements, and by the way he or she treats others. For each of the attributes listed in the center of the page, write the name of one character from the novel who has this trait, and the name of a character who does **not** have this trait. After each character's name, give an example of an action or statement which proves you have properly evaluated the character.

Has This Trait		Doesn't Have This Trait
	tells the truth	
	keeps promises	
	considers consequences of actions	
	sacrifices for others	
	listens to others without pre-judging them	
	is a good person	
	is kind and caring	

© Novel Units, Inc.

Name _____

A Tree Grows in Brooklyn
Activity #13 • Comprehension
Use During and After Reading

Conflict

The **conflict** of a story is the struggle between two people or two forces. There are three main types of conflict: person vs. person, person vs. nature or society, and person vs. self.

Directions: The characters in *A Tree Grows in Brooklyn* experience some conflicts in the story. In the chart below, list the names of three major characters. In the space provided, list a conflict each character experiences. Then explain how each conflict is resolved in the story.

Character:

Conflict	Resolution

Character:

Conflict	Resolution

Character:

Conflict	Resolution

Name _____

A Tree Grows in Brooklyn
Activity #14 • Literary Analysis
Use After Reading

Directions: Complete the graph below.

Graphing Plot Lines

Characters

Setting

Problem

Climax

Resolution

Building Action

Beginning

Name _____

A Tree Grows in Brooklyn
Activity #15 • Literary Analysis
Use After Reading

Story Pyramid

Directions: Using the pyramid, write words or phrases to summarize the story.

Line 1: One word that gives the setting

Line 2: Two words that identify the two main characters (in order of their appearance)

Line 3: Three words that explain the problem

Line 4: Two words that describe character #1; two words that describe character #2

Line 5: Two characters that interact with character #1; three characters that interact with character #2

Line 6: Six words that explain the resolution of the conflict

Line 7: Seven words that summarize your impresssion of the book

1 _____

2 _____ _____

3 _____ _____ _____

4 _____ _____ _____ _____

5 _____ _____ _____ _____ _____

6 _____ _____ _____ _____ _____ _____

7 _____ _____ _____ _____ _____ _____ _____

Name _____

A Tree Grows in Brooklyn
Activity #16 • Literary Analysis
Use After Reading

Thematic Analysis

Directions: Choose a theme from the book to be the focus of your word web. Complete the web and then answer the question in each starred box.

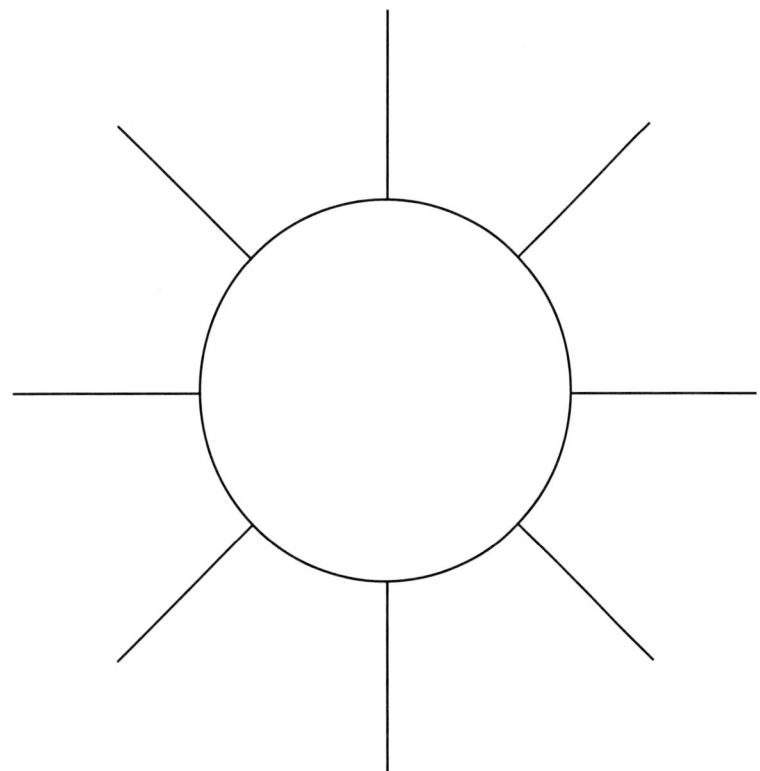

 What is the author's main message?

 What did you learn from the book?

Name _____

A Tree Grows in Brooklyn
Quiz #1
Chapters 1–6, Pages 5–54

A. Short Answer: Write brief answers to the following on a separate sheet of paper.

1. Identify the setting and explain why it is important to the plot.
2. How do Francie and Neeley start their Saturdays? How do their Saturdays end?
3. What is significant about the Tree of Heaven?
4. From what two books must Francie and Neeley read each night?
5. Give two reasons to which Johnny attributes his drinking.

B. True/False

_____ 6. Katie Nolan will not allow her children to waste anything.

_____ 7. Johnny Nolan loves his family but does not feel he is good enough for them.

_____ 8. Francie doesn't trust Aunt Sissy because of her bad reputation.

_____ 9. Sissy's greatest heartache is her inability to give birth to a healthy child.

_____ 10. In spite of their poverty, the Nolans will never pawn Katie's wedding ring.

C. Open-Ended Comprehension: On the lines below, explain what the library symbolizes to Francie and describe her "reading plan."

_____

_____

_____

_____

_____

_____

_____

_____

Name _____

A Tree Grows in Brooklyn
Quiz #2
Chapters 7–14, Pages 57–123

A. True/False

____ 1. Sissy asks her first husband to leave because he is unable to father living children.

____ 2. Johnny Nolan and his three brothers become singing waiters.

____ 3. Johnny loses his job as school custodian because he stays with Katie during Francie's birth.

____ 4. Sissy helps Johnny recover from delirium tremens.

____ 5. Francie immediately makes friends when the family moves to Lorimer Street.

B. Short Answer: Write brief answers to the following on a separate sheet of paper.

6. Briefly describe Johnny and Katie's first year of marriage.

7. Identify one attribute Francie inherits from her father and another she inherits from her mother.

8. What effect does Neeley's birth have on Johnny and Francie? Why?

9. Identify Sissy's two great failings. What does this cause her to do?

10. Why does the Nolan family move away from Lorimer Street?

C. Open-Ended Comprehension: On the lines below, explain the statement, "[The Rommely women] were made out of thin invisible steel."

_____

_____

_____

_____

_____

_____

_____

Name _____

A Tree Grows in Brooklyn
Quiz #3
Chapters 15–32, Pages 127–248

A. Identification: Match each character with the correct description.

____ 1. Miss Lizzie Tynmore
____ 2. doctor at the clinic
____ 3. Johnny Nolan
____ 4. Sissy
____ 5. Francie
____ 6. Katie
____ 7. Mr. Morton
____ 8. Sergeant McShane
____ 9. Joanna
____ 10. "teacher's pet"

a. protects her children with home remedies
b. finds a way for Francie to attend another school
c. victim of stone-throwing women
d. gives Katie piano lessons
e. spits in Francie's face
f. takes up for Francie with a harsh teacher
g. replaces Francie's tickets at a political picnic
h. humiliates Francie by referring to her as dirty
i. gold and silver sun-splash in a great muddy river
j. lies to get a pie and a doll

B. Open-Ended Comprehension: On the lines below, explain the irony of the nurse's reaction to Francie at the clinic.

_____
_____
_____
_____
_____
_____
_____
_____

Name _____

A Tree Grows in Brooklyn
Quiz #4
Chapters 33–42, Pages 249–360

A. True/False

____ 1. Katie kills the sexual predator who attacks Francie.

____ 2. Sissy gives birth to Sarah.

____ 3. McShane takes Katie to the hospital after Johnny is found unconscious.

____ 4. Mr. McGarrity helps the Nolan family by hiring Francie and Neeley.

____ 5. Johnny's death certificate lists "acute alcoholism and pneumonia" as his cause of death.

____ 6. At her graduation, Francie receives flowers from Johnny.

B. Sequencing: Using the letters *a–e*, list the following events in the order in which they occur in the novel.

____ 7. Johnny is kicked out of the Waiters' Union.

____ 8. Katie tells Johnny she is pregnant again.

____ 9. Johnny dies.

____ 10. Francie writes realistic stories about Johnny.

____ 11. Johnny quits drinking.

C. Open-Ended Comprehension: On the lines below, explain what Johnny's family symbolizes to Mr. McGarrity.

_____
_____
_____
_____
_____
_____

Name _____

A Tree Grows in Brooklyn
Quiz #5
Chapters 43–56, Pages 363–493

A. Fill in the Blanks

1. Katie tells her children that only _____ will be able to go to high school the year after eighth-grade graduation.

2. After a confrontation with Katie, Francie compares their family to _____ _____.

3. The "musical" shouting fight between the Germans and the Irish symbolizes _____.

4. Francie is reluctant to tell her mother about her possible promotion at the Bureau because _____.

5. Ben Blake helps Francie with her college courses by _____ _____.

B. Short Answer: Write brief answers to the following on a separate sheet of paper.

6. What do Neeley and Francie do with their first week's wages?
7. Why is the New Year's toast significant to Katie?
8. How does Sissy give birth to a healthy baby?
9. How does Lee Rhynor break Francie's heart?
10. How are the Nolans' financial worries resolved?

C. Open-Ended Comprehension: On the lines below, explain how Katie responds to Francie's revelation of her last evening with Lee Rhynor. Why is her response significant?

_____
_____
_____
_____
_____
_____

Name _____

A Tree Grows in Brooklyn
Novel Test • Level One

A. Identification: Match each character with the correct description.

____ 1. Francie Nolan   a. resourceful, protective, hardened by poverty
____ 2. Johnny Nolan   b. intelligent, realistic, supportive friend
____ 3. Katie Nolan   c. perceptive, optimistic, creative, determined
____ 4. Neeley Nolan   d. humiliates student by calling her stories "sordid"
____ 5. Aunt Sissy   e. scheming soldier who breaks a girl's heart
____ 6. Aunt Evy   f. kind, loyal, generous policeman
____ 7. Miss Garnder   g. imaginative, talented, compassionate alcoholic
____ 8. Sergeant Michael McShane   h. has two great failings: lover and mother
____ 9. Lee Rhynor   i. musical, good-looking, favorite child
____ 10. Ben Blake   j. takes a "man's job" when her husband leaves her

B. Multiple Choice: Choose the BEST answer.

____ 11. Residents of the Williamsburg neighborhood of Brooklyn represent
   (a) a crime-ridden area
   (b) America's upper class
   (c) the despair of homelessness
   (d) immigrants seeking a better life in America

____ 12. Francie first sees the Tree of Heaven
   (a) in her yard
   (b) in the schoolyard
   (c) after she moves to Lorimer Street
   (d) when she starts to work in New York City

____ 13. Francie plans to read
   (a) the Bible in one year
   (b) books written in different languages
   (c) one Shakespearean play each month
   (d) one book each day in alphabetical order

____ 14. No matter how much the family needs money, they would never pawn
   (a) the baby's crib
   (b) Johnny's pearl studs
   (c) Katie's wedding ring
   (d) their collection of books

Name _____

A Tree Grows in Brooklyn
Novel Test • Level One
page 2

____ 15. Katie initially falls in love with Johnny because of his
    (a) political ideas
    (b) dark, curly hair
    (c) high-paying job
    (d) ability to sing and dance

____ 16. Katie's father never forgives her for marrying Johnny because
    (a) Johnny beat him up
    (b) she is his favorite daughter
    (c) they eloped without telling him
    (d) he thinks she should keep working to support him

____ 17. From her father and mother, respectively, Francie inherits
    (a) musical ability/beauty
    (b) sentimentality/softness
    (c) writing skills/storytelling ability
    (d) tendency to drink/forgiving heart

____ 18. When Johnny suffers from delirium tremens, Katie
    (a) asks Sissy for help
    (b) sends him to his mother
    (c) threatens to divorce him
    (d) seeks her mother's advice

____ 19. Francie is lonely when the family moves to Lorimer Street because
    (a) few children live nearby
    (b) her mother won't let her go outside
    (c) she is too bossy to the other children
    (d) she doesn't know how to make friends with the other girls

____ 20. The Nolans decide to move away from Lorimer Street because
    (a) Johnny wants a new start
    (b) Katie is looking for a better school
    (c) Sissy inadvertently causes problems
    (d) they are about to get evicted for not paying their rent

____ 21. The relationship between Katie Nolan and Lizzy Tynmore is best described as
    (a) destined to fail
    (b) mutually dependent
    (c) hostile but necessary
    (d) similar to that of mother/daughter

Name _____

A Tree Grows in Brooklyn
Novel Test • Level One
page 3

____ 22. The doctor at the free clinic humiliates Francie by
    (a) refusing to treat her
    (b) talking about her "filth"
    (c) complaining about charity patients
    (d) referring to her father's alcoholism

____ 23. When Francie has an "accident" at school, Sissy
    (a) shames her
    (b) takes her home
    (c) tells Katie about it
    (d) confronts the teacher

____ 24. Johnny arranges for Francie to attend a better school by
    (a) taking her there each day
    (b) telling Katie they must move
    (c) telling the principal she is too intelligent for the old school
    (d) telling the principal she lives in a house in a nearby neighborhood

____ 25. Francie tells her first "planned lie"
    (a) to get a pumpkin pie
    (b) to get Neeley out of trouble
    (c) because she hasn't done her homework
    (d) because she doesn't want to get spanked

____ 26. When a sexual predator grabs Francie, Katie
    (a) kills him
    (b) attacks him with a knife
    (c) shoots him but does not kill him
    (d) runs into the street to find a policeman

____ 27. Johnny's lowest point of despair comes
    (a) right after he has the delirium tremens
    (b) when McShane brings him home drunk
    (c) when Katie tells him she is pregnant again
    (d) when he is thrown out of the Waiters' Union

____ 28. Katie insists that the cause of Johnny's death be stated as
    (a) heart disease
    (b) hypothermia
    (c) pneumonia
    (d) pneumonia and alcoholism

Name _____

A Tree Grows in Brooklyn
Novel Test • Level One
page 4

_____ 29. McGarrity helps the family after Johnny's death by
(a) paying their rent
(b) hiring Francie and Neeley
(c) paying for the funeral expenses
(d) returning the $38.00 Johnny overpaid him

_____ 30. Miss Garnder refuses to allow Francie's play to be used for graduation because
(a) it is too realistic
(b) it contains too much fantasy
(c) she thinks Francie is disrespectful
(d) Francie doesn't know how to write well

_____ 31. At her eighth-grade graduation, Francie receives flowers from
(a) Evy
(b) her father
(c) her mother
(d) Neeley

_____ 32. When Francie and Neeley receive their first week's wages for their full-time jobs, they
(a) put half in a bank
(b) give all the money to Katie
(c) give half the money to Katie
(d) save it to buy Christmas gifts

_____ 33. Francie initially does not tell Katie about the chance to make $20.00 a week because
(a) she wants to secure the job first
(b) Neeley tells her to keep it a secret
(c) her boss tells her not to tell anyone
(d) she is afraid that Katie won't let her go to high school

_____ 34. Francie loses her job at the Model Press Clipping Bureau as an indirect result of
(a) her desire to attend college
(b) more convenient methods of filing
(c) Katie's marriage to Sergeant McShane
(d) the United States' entry into World War I

_____ 35. Sissy's baby, Stephen Aaron, lives because
(a) of better prenatal care
(b) of an expert mid-wife
(c) of a good doctor and a hospital
(d) she carries the baby to full-term

Name _____

A Tree Grows in Brooklyn
Novel Test • Level One
page 5

____ 36. When Francie's heart is broken, Katie's heart aches because
    (a) Francie cries for her father
    (b) Francie has betrayed her trust
    (c) she can no longer protect her from heartache
    (d) she remembers the heartbreak of a failed relationship

____ 37. Before he marries Katie, McShane
    (a) asks to adopt Annie Laurie
    (b) buys Katie a beautiful ring
    (c) gives Katie's sister Evy $200.00
    (d) asks Francie and Neeley to call him "Father"

____ 38. Francie plans to attend the University of Michigan because
    (a) Ben Blake chooses it for her
    (b) she wants to leave New York
    (c) she wants to get rid of her Brooklyn accent
    (d) it is the only college to which she is accepted

____ 39. The Nolans' religious heritage is
    (a) Hindu
    (b) Jewish
    (c) Protestant
    (d) Roman Catholic

____ 40. *A Tree Grows in Brooklyn* is
    (a) a biography
    (b) historical fiction
    (c) semi-autobiographical
    (d) a late twentieth-century publication

C. Open-Ended Short Answer Questions: Respond to the following on a separate sheet of paper. Support your answers with evidence from the novel.

(a) Explain the importance of setting to the novel.

(b) Identify one type of conflict and explain its development and resolution within the novel.

D. Essay: On a separate sheet of paper, complete one of the following in a well-developed essay. Cite specific evidence from the novel to support your answer.

(a) List details of at least three events in Francie's life that develop the theme of "loss of innocence."

(b) Discuss the causes, effects, and resolutions of the Nolans' poverty.

Name _____

A Tree Grows in Brooklyn
Novel Test • Level Two

A. Identification

1. List three characteristics of Francie Nolan and identify a time when she feels fear, humiliation, compassion, and sorrow.

List two characteristics for each of the following characters and explain his or her significance in Francie's life.

2. Johnny
3. Katie
4. Neeley
5. Sissy
6. Miss Garnder
7. Ben Blake
8. Lee Rhynor
9. Mary Rommely
10. Sergeant Michael McShane

B. Multiple Choice: Choose the BEST answer.

_____ 11. Which of the following is NOT one of Johnny's rationales for drinking?
(a) He hates his wife and children.
(b) His responsibilities overwhelm him.
(c) He doesn't think he will ever be successful.
(d) His dream of becoming a real singer never came true.

_____ 12. Mary Rommely encourages Katie to do all BUT which one of the following after Francie's birth?
(a) teach Francie about Heaven
(b) start saving to buy some land
(c) teach Francie that supernatural creatures do not exist
(d) read one page of the Bible and one page of Shakespeare to Francie each day until she learns to read

Name _____

A Tree Grows in Brooklyn
Novel Test • Level Two
page 2

_____ 13. "They were made out of thin invisible steel" refers to
   (a) the Rommely women
   (b) Johnny Nolan's ancestors
   (c) the teachers at Francie's first school
   (d) the girders on the Williamsburg Bridge

_____ 14. Johnny loses his job as school custodian because
   (a) he defies the authorities
   (b) his neglect causes the pipes to burst
   (c) he stays with Katie when Francie is born
   (d) the Board of Education discovers his alcoholism

_____ 15. While helping Johnny through an episode of delirium tremens, Sissy reveals her
   (a) lust for him
   (b) counseling skills
   (c) maternal instinct
   (d) own battle with alcoholism

_____ 16. Evidence of Johnny's love for Francie includes all BUT which one of the following?
   (a) treating her infected arm
   (b) sending flowers to her graduation
   (c) arranging for her to attend a different school
   (d) confronting the teacher after Francie's "accident"

_____ 17. Which one of the following is NOT a result of Francie's experience with a sexual predator?
   (a) Katie shoots him but does not kill him.
   (b) He confesses that he murdered a little girl.
   (c) Johnny washes away her "shame" with carbolic acid.
   (d) Johnny takes Francie to the hospital to assess whether she has been molested.

_____ 18. McGarrity comes to the aid of the Nolan family after Johnny's death because
   (a) he misses Johnny
   (b) Johnny had overpaid him by $38.00
   (c) he wants Katie to fall in love with him
   (d) he feels guilty for having given Johnny liquor

_____ 19. Before his marriage to Katie, McShane does all BUT which of the following?
   (a) gives Katie $1,000.00
   (b) asks to adopt Annie Laurie
   (c) asks Francie and Neeley to call him "Father"
   (d) offers to pay Francie's and Neeley's college tuition

© Novel Units, Inc.

Name _____

A Tree Grows in Brooklyn
Novel Test • Level Two
page 3

____ 20. Francie does all BUT which of the following on the last Saturday in her old home?
(a) goes to the library
(b) visits her father's grave
(c) pays for a doll at Cheap Charlie's
(d) asks Neeley to sing "Molly Malone"

C. Identifying Quotations: Identify the speaker of each of the following quotes and explain its context.

21. "Maybe the pigeon wanted to get away from its relatives."
22. "Our family used to be like a strong cup."
23. "I'm sure you'll stop writing those sordid little stories."
24. "I guess being needed is almost as good as being loved."
25. "I will tell you the truth as a woman. It would have been a very beautiful thing."

D. Open-Ended Short Answer Questions: Respond to the following on a separate sheet of paper. Support your answers with evidence from the novel.

26. Explain why the Tree of Heaven is a metaphor for Francie's life.
27. Explain what the library symbolizes to Francie.
28. Explain the oxymoron, "Sissy was bad. But she was good."
29. Explain why Francie's experience at the free clinic is a significant step in her "loss of innocence."
30. Trace the steps leading to Johnny's final decline and death.

E. Essay: On a separate sheet of paper, complete one of the following in a well-developed essay. Cite specific evidence from the novel to support your answer.

(a) Explain the symbolism of two of the following: Johnny's pearl studs, the tin-can bank, Johnny's Union button, the Williamsburg Bridge, Florry Wendy.

(b) Write a character analysis of Francie Nolan. Include what she is like at the beginning of the novel, circumstances that mold her, and what she is like at the end.

Name _____

A Tree Grows in Brooklyn
Alternative Assessment

Directions: For items #1–#4, write a well-developed paragraph on a separate sheet of paper, citing examples from the book. Respond to two items from #5–#8.

1. Explain how the novel correlates with World War I.
2. Identify and explain at least three steps of Francie's coming-of-age.
3. Identify and explain one of the following types of conflict in the novel: person vs. person, person vs. society, person vs. self.
4. Apply the following quote to the life of Johnny Nolan: "It is not easy for men to rise whose qualities are thwarted by poverty" (Juvenal, Satires, I, I. 164).
5. Write a metaphorical poem of at least 12 lines about poverty as it is portrayed in the novel.
6. Write a "This Is Your Life" feature article about Francie Nolan ten years after the novel's end.
7. Write a ballad that tells the story of Francie and the two young men in her life (Lee Rhynor and Ben Blake).
8. Pretend you are Francie and it has been a few years since you have moved away from Brooklyn. Write a letter to Katie, updating her on all aspects of your life.

Answer Key

Activities #1–#3: Answers will vary.

Activity #4: 1. consternation 2. vacuous 3. lassitude 4. conscripted 5. Purgatory 6. beguiling 7. impotence 8. latent 9. enigma

Activity #5: Puzzles will vary.

Activity #6: Answers will vary. Example: Vocabulary Word—contemptuously; Definition—showing lack of respect or reverence; Synonym—scornfully; Antonym—respectfully; Pronunciation—con temp' tu ous ly; Part of Speech—adverb; Sentence—The arrogant man treated his employees contemptuously.

Activity #7: Answers will vary.

Study Guide

Book One: Chapters 1–3, pp. 5–38: 1. early 1900s, Williamsburg neighborhood of Brooklyn (p. 5) 2. Francie: imaginative, loves to read; Neeley: youngest child, likes baseball (throughout) 3. Tree of Heaven; Answers will vary (p. 6). 4. selling junk to Carney, getting treats from Cheap Charlie or Gimpy, buying food for their mother, reading or playing; Answers will vary (pp. 6–26). 5. Johnny: handsome, talented, unreliable, alcoholic, singing waiter; Katie: reliable, pretty, thrifty, janitress (pp. 12–14, 33–38) 6. play for the Brooklyn baseball team; Answers will vary (p. 21). 7. loves it and thinks it's beautiful; wishes she would look at her; read a book a day in alphabetical order (pp. 22–24) 8. works sporadically; Union assures him of getting fair wages; "Molly Malone"; waits for him, likes him better than Katie, is attentive to him (pp. 33–36, throughout) 9. no education or chance to succeed, overwhelming responsibilities; Answers will vary (pp. 34–35). 10. pearl studs, golden collar button; Answers will vary (p. 37).

Book One: Chapters 4–6, pp. 39–54: 1. the Nolans' neighbors; dying from consumption; works in a glove factory, works on her costumes, works on Frank (pp. 39–40) 2. has the feeling something (death) is hidden in the costumes; Answers will vary (p. 41). 3. wild with men, black eyes and hair, clear complexion, works in a rubber factory; Francie's favorite aunt (pp. 42–43) 4. to confession; Answers will vary (pp. 48–49). 5. one page from the Bible and one from Shakespeare (p. 51) 6. excited, love to hear about his work, grateful for the food he brings; Answers will vary (pp. 51–52). 7. Answers will vary.

Book Two: Chapters 7–10, pp. 57–97: 1. when Hildy O'Dair, Johnny's girlfriend, arranges a blind date for Katie and a friend of Johnny's and the two couples go dancing; strongly attracted to each other (pp. 57–61) 2. Thomas Rommely: cruel, vindictive, selfish; Mary Rommely: kind, compassionate, loving (pp. 61–62) 3. tells their teacher they must speak nothing but English; Answers will vary (p. 63). 4. a fireman; 14; four; All are born dead (pp. 64–65). 5. two; eight; All die; Answers will vary (p. 66). 6. Willie Flittman; loves him but likes to make fun of him; a good education (especially in music) and respectability (pp. 67–69) 7. the Rommely women; Answers will vary (p. 69). 8. four; singing waiters; All die before the age of 35 (pp. 70–71). 9. father: weaknesses, passion for beauty, sentimentality; mother: softness, half of her invisible steel; avid reader, observant, her unique day-to-day life and soul (pp. 72–73) 10. gets drunk and loses his job; financial struggle (pp. 77–78, 80) 11. read one page of Shakespeare and one page of the Bible each day, tell Francie legends, teach Francie about God, save to own a bit of land (pp. 83–85) 12. Neeley most important in her affections, Johnny second, Francie third (pp. 95–96)

Book Two: Chapters 11–14, pp. 98–123: 1. gets drunk for three days; has delirium tremens (p. 98) 2. gives him periodic sips of whiskey, comforts him, holds him while he sleeps; nag him; Answers will vary (pp. 99–104). 3. great lover, great mother (p. 100) 4. Katie's shame over Johnny's drinking spree; works fairly steadily, doesn't drink as much (pp. 104, 107) 5. avoid her because she talks funny; has shouting match with one girl, cries; Answers will vary (pp. 109–110). 6. imaginary friends, plays games by herself; becomes interested in street musicians (pp. 111–113) 7. takes a child's bike without permission to give the children a ride, allows the children to play with a box of condoms—they open it and display its contents outside; Sissy is banned from the Nolans' home (pp. 117–121). 8. so Neeley can go with her and they can help each other (pp. 122–123) 9. will be his last; Answers will vary (p. 123).

Book Three: Chapters 15–24, pp. 127–189: 1. spits in her face; Answers will vary; sits alone in the cellar until the hurt stops (pp. 128–129) 2. Purgatory; all the vile things at the bottom (p. 130) 3. A former tenant leaves it in the apartment; Miss Lizzie Tynmore; spends one hour cleaning the Tynmores' home; Katie shows them what she learns (pp. 139–142). 4. makes derogatory statements about her "filth"; humiliates her, tells the doctor not to tell Neeley he is dirty; She is from the same poor background (pp. 146–147). 5. expectation—thinks she'll learn to read and write the first day of school, reality—learns reading and writing is a step-by-step process; expectation—thinks she'll have her own desk, reality—has to share a desk meant for only one; expectation—thinks she will get her own supplies, reality—must return her pencil at end of each day; expectation—teacher will like her, reality—likes only affluent students; Answers will vary (pp. 151–152). 6. wets her pants; Teacher always allows her to leave the room if she needs to (pp. 153–158). 7. vermin: scrubs Francie's head with strong soap and brushes kerosene into it, disease: makes each of them wear a bag containing garlic around their necks; Everyone avoids them, and they never get sick or have lice (pp. 160–162). 8. likes the routine and feels safe there; discovers a world where she will never be lonely (pp. 163, 166–167) 9. picks a house number in the neighborhood and writes the principal a letter stating that Francie will be living there; everyone treated more equally (pp. 173–174) 10. thinks politicians take care of their constituents; thinks it won't happen but Katie will vote his way if it does (pp. 179–181) 11. gambles them away; Sergeant Michael McShane; Answers will vary (pp. 182–184).

Book Three: Chapters 25–32, pp. 190–248: 1. Life becomes too much for him; decides to be a better father, work hard, and teach his children things (pp. 190–192) 2. to get a small pumpkin pie; doesn't enjoy the pie and learns to tell the truth but write the story the way she thinks things should be (pp. 197–199) 3. by winning it from a salesman—he throws it at them and they don't fall down; Answers will vary (pp. 202–204). 4. sees their excitement but also the filth and dirt of the neighborhood; determines they must get an education to escape the poverty that creates this kind of situation (pp. 206–208) 5. wants a doll given away by a rich little girl; Answers will vary; real first name is Mary (pp. 211–212, 215) 6. Henny Gaddis dies, Neeley grows taller than her, she discovers that her mother is sometimes wrong and that some of the things she loves about her father are considered comical to others, discovers the "catch" in the "North Pole" game, the theater seems unrealistic; Answers will vary (pp. 216–220). 7. thinks they're growing up ignorant of the ocean; Tilly; Johnny and Tilly fall into the water, the children get terrible sunburns and nausea, the fish he buys to take home are rotten, Tilly throws up all over his only suit (pp. 221–228). 8. has an illegitimate child; taunt her, throw stones at her; a stone hits her baby; feels sad and guilty for not smiling at Joanna and decides she cannot trust women (pp. 230–238) 9. often "sick" from drinking excessively and doesn't work much, family is often hungry and has to spend all the money from their tin-can bank; says she is curious about sex; Answers will vary (pp. 243–248).

Book Three: Chapters 33–37, pp. 249–299: 1. borrows a gun from his friend; Answers will vary (pp. 252–254). 2. in the hallway by the stairs; Katie shoots him but doesn't kill him, other people beat him; uses carbolic acid to scrub the spot on her leg where the predator's penis touched her and tells her it was all a dream (pp. 254–259) 3. from an expectant unwed mother; shut her up in a dark room and feed her only bread and water; Answers will vary (pp. 266–268). 4. thinks she's played a dirty trick on her husband; He's happy because now he won't have to worry about Sissy leaving him (p. 271). 5. Answers will vary; quits drinking but acts like he is, doesn't work, speak to his family, or sing, stays out late at night, hands tremble, looks very old; Answers will vary (pp. 272–275). 6. He is thrown out for being a drunk and told they'll never give him another job; his Union button (pp. 279–280) 7. acute alcoholism and pneumonia; just pneumonia; $175.00 (pp. 284–285) 8. Katie tells her the neighbors think they won't do so because he wasn't a good father; forces herself to stay by the coffin so everyone will know he was a good father (pp. 288–289) 9. his barber cup, signet ring, two waiter's aprons (p. 292) 10. that she is pregnant (p. 293) 11. walk around bewildered, sit close together, weep long and quietly, and talk about why he had to die; urges them to go for a walk, serves them hot chocolate when they return (pp. 294–297)

Book Three: Chapters 38–42, pp. 300–360: 1. thinks she needs to go to work; insists they can make it until she graduates from eighth grade; have Francie drop out of school and get her working papers (pp. 300–303) 2. loved Johnny and his stories about his family, wishes he had a family like Johnny's; talks to them about Johnny and gives Francie and Neeley jobs after school (pp. 305–311) 3. McGarrity gave them back pieces of Johnny when he talked about him but now has no more of Johnny in him (p. 316). 4. writes realistic stories about Johnny rather than nature and her impressions; thinks she should write about beautiful things instead of ugly subjects such as poverty, starvation, and drunkenness; Answers will vary (pp. 321–323). 5. lashes out at her and tells her never to use that word about her family again; Answers will vary; starts to write a "pretty" novel but burns it (pp. 323–328) 6. cleans the flat, cooks their supper, wipes her face with a cool cloth, reads to her; to protect her from Katie's agony when the baby is born (pp. 333–342) 7. Annie Laurie; Johnny sang a song by that name (p. 344). 8. flowers from Johnny; Johnny had given Sissy the card and money to order them before his death; cries (pp. 351–352) 9. knows they have more education than she has but thinks it isn't enough, has gotten them through the eighth grade but can't do more for them, hopes to do better for Laurie (pp. 356–357) 10. 20 cents; wants them to feel rich for once; wants to shout out that Mama is somebody (p. 359) 11. Answers will vary.

Book Four: Chapters 43–46, pp. 363–407: 1. Francie: floral factory, Neeley: errand boy in brokerage house; taunt her; She laughs at the utility boy (pp. 364–366). 2. trade the old bills for new ones and take it all to Katie; cries; Answers will vary (pp. 368–371). 3. two weeks; works for a clipping bureau (pp. 372–374) 4. city reader; wants to talk it over with Katie before giving an answer (pp. 381–382) 5. Only Neeley can go to high school in the fall; Neeley doesn't want to go, and Francie is angry because she wants to go; Neeley will never go if Katie doesn't make him, but Francie is determined enough to go later (pp. 384–386). 6. because they are so much alike; a cup that was once strong but is now cracked; Answers will vary (pp. 386–387). 7. enough money for Christmas gifts, plenty of food, warm flat; can talk about him without so much grief (pp. 388–393) 8. fir; Annie; Answers will vary (pp. 393–395). 9. Germans drown them out singing a song in German; Answers will vary (p. 401). 10. to test them and see if they have Johnny's tendency toward alcoholism; Neeley pours his down the sink; Francie thinks a vanilla ice-cream soda is better; Answers will vary (pp. 402–403).

Book Four: Chapters 47–54, pp. 408–472: 1. He has died, they were never divorced, and she gets his $500.00 life insurance policy; uses all the money on his funeral (pp. 410–413) 2. He divorced Sissy and is married again; get married legally (pp. 414–415) 3. Steve; Answers will vary (p. 417). 4. "WAR"; front page of newspaper, new 1917 penny, her fingerprints underlined with her lipstick, copy of a poem, lock of her hair; Answers will vary (pp. 419–421). 5. government agents arrest one of the main clients as a German spy, business slows down due to war and draft; Answers will vary (pp. 422–423). 6. sends and receives messages on a teletype machine; night schedule makes it possible to attend college classes in the daytime (pp. 426–428) 7. a young man whom she meets in the college bookstore; tutors her, checks her assignments, prepares her for finals; friends; Answers will vary (pp. 423–437). 8. have a doctor and go to the hospital; are stunned; baby lives (pp. 438–440) 9. Anita talks her into going out with him; falls in love with him (pp. 448–454) 10. spend the night with him; refuses; to wait for him (pp. 458–460) 11. Lee married his fiancée the next day; receives a letter from his wife; cries and goes to Katie; Answers will vary (pp. 461–463). 12. as a mother, feels it would have been wrong to spend the night with Lee, but as a woman, feels it would have been a beautiful experience; Answers will vary (pp. 463–464). 13. will marry him because he is a good man and she would be proud to be his wife; adopt Laurie, pay college tuition for Francie and Neeley (pp. 469–471)

Book Five: Chapters 55–56, pp. 475–493: 1. University of Michigan in Ann Arbor; Ben Blake (pp. 477–478) 2. ambitious, helpful, intelligent, considerate; his high-school ring; as a promise of another ring in five years if they love each other; thinks he's wonderful but still thinks of Lee (pp. 478–481) 3. $1,000.00; gives it to Evy; It is the amount of Willie's insurance policy—he's "as good as dead" (pp. 482–483). 4. Carney's junk shop to buy all the "picks," the park, her old school, the house whose address she claimed, McGarrity's former saloon, library (pp. 483–487) 5. crucifix and confirmation picture of her and Neeley, Johnny's waiter's aprons and shaving cup, doll named Mary, box that had held her ten pennies, her small "library," her diary, her "time capsule," four stories about Johnny; Answers will vary (pp. 487–489). 6. irons his shirt; sings and calls her "Prima Donna" (pp. 489–490) 7. Florry sitting on the fire escape reading, the tree; Answers will vary (pp. 492–493).

Activity #8: Cause #1—Neither Katie nor Johnny has more than a sixth-grade education; Both quit school to start to work. Cause #2—Katie has Francie less than a year after getting married; Johnny gets drunk, neglects the school, and loses his job. Cause #3—Johnny's alcoholism becomes increasingly severe; He only works sporadically. Cause #4—Johnny dies; Katie, pregnant again, cannot work enough to provide for them.

Activity #9: Katie Nolan: pretty, reliable, industrious, protects her children, loves her husband in spite of his drinking; Johnny Nolan: handsome, weak, talented, overwhelmed by responsibilities, alcoholic; Neeley Nolan: amusing, cooperative, Francie's younger brother, confidant, companion; Aunt Sissy: has bad reputation because she is "wild with men," good-hearted, compassionate, generous, endures heartache of losing ten children; Miss Garnder: meticulous, controlling, expects students to write "beauty" rather than "realism"; Sergeant McShane: kind, generous, faithful, dependable, patiently waits for Katie; Lee Rhynor: manipulative, handsome, deceptive, "uses" a girl and casts her aside; Ben Blake: handsome, intelligent, helpful, goal-oriented, cautious

Activity #10: Francie Nolan—happy and carefree in spite of poverty; (1) Neeley is born—eventually feels unsure of Katie's love (2) a schoolgirl spits in her face—humiliated, sad (3) starts school and learns to read—thrilled, satisfied (4) her father dies—sad, lonely (5) has to go to work instead of high school—disheartened, unsure (6) falls in love and is jilted—heartbroken, hopeless; prepares to leave the old neighborhood and go to college—excited, expectant, hopeful

Activity #11: Center: Francie; Johnny: Francie loves him intensely; Johnny tries to protect her from harm. Katie: Francie admires her but knows she favors Neeley; Katie needs her financially and, when in labor, emotionally. Sissy: Francie adores her in spite of her bad reputation; Sissy makes her feel important and confronts a teacher when she mistreats Francie. Ben Blake: Francie really likes and respects him but is not sure she loves him; Ben tutors her, helps her, and loves her.

Activity #12: tells the truth—Katie Nolan, does not—Lee Rhynor; keeps promises—Ben Blake, does not—Lee Rhynor; considers consequences—Sergeant McShane, does not—Sissy; sacrifices for others—Katie, does not—Willie Flittman; listens to others without prejudging them—Mary Rommely, does not—Miss Garnder; good person—Johnny Nolan, is not—Thomas Rommely; kind and caring—Sissy, is not—Miss Briggs; Answers will vary.

Activity #13: Character: Francie, Conflict: person vs. person—Miss Garnder denigrates Francie's writing, Resolution: Francie quits turning in work, burns the "beautiful" novel she starts; Character: Johnny Nolan, Conflict: person vs. self—will to be responsible, emotions, and alcoholism, Resolution:

Johnny dies; Character: Katie Nolan, Conflict: person vs. society—family's survival and poverty, Resolution: children start to work, agrees to marry McShane

Activity #14: Characters: Francie, Katie, Johnny, Neeley, Aunt Sissy, Sergeant McShane, Evy, Mary Rommely; Setting: Williamsburg, Brooklyn, 1900–1918; Problem: the Nolan family struggles against poverty; Beginning (sequentially): Katie and Johnny marry young. Building Action: (1) Johnny loses his job when Francie is born. (2) Neeley is born a year after Francie. (3) Johnny works only sporadically and drinks excessively. (4) Katie must work as a janitress to provide most of their needs. (5) The children start school and experience prejudice because of their poverty. (6) Johnny dies. (7) The children must go to work after eighth grade. (8) Francie takes some college courses. Climax: Katie accepts Sergeant McShane's marriage proposal. Resolution: The family prepares to leave their old home. Francie prepares to leave for college.

Activity #15: 1. Brooklyn 2. Francie, Katie 3. family faces poverty 4. imaginative, devoted; reliable, resourceful 5. Aunt Sissy, Lee Rhynor; Johnny Nolan, Neeley, Mary Rommely 6. Katie accepts Sergeant McShane's marriage proposal. 7. Answers will vary.

Activity #16: Theme: coming of age—growing up as a child selling junk for a few pennies; learning to frugally buy food; starting school and experiencing the social "caste" system; dealing with her father's death; conflicting with Katie over school; having to go to work to support the family; falling in love and having her heart broken; attaining her dream of attending college; Main message: Each person is the sum of his/her experiences. With perseverance and the support of one's family, the challenges of childhood and adolescence can not only be overcome but can mold us into strong and empathetic human beings. What you learned: Answers will vary.

Quiz #1: A. 1. Williamsburg section of Brooklyn, 1900–1918; representative of poverty of Nolan family (p. 5) 2. selling junk to Carney; Neeley playing ball with his friends, Francie reading (pp. 6–7, 18–21) 3. grows in spite of bad conditions, sprouts even after being cut down (p. 6) 4. Bible, Shakespeare (p. 51) 5. responsibilities he can't handle, doesn't have a chance to succeed (pp. 34–35) **B.** 6. F (p. 14) 7. T (p. 33) 8. F (p. 42) 9. T (pp. 42–43, implied) 10. F (p. 37) **C.** Answers will vary. Refer to the scoring rubric on p. 46 of this guide.

Quiz #2: A. 1. T (p. 65) 2. T (p. 71) 3. F (pp. 77–80) 4. T (pp. 99–101) 5. F (pp. 109–110) **B.** 6. happy, have fun working together, have sufficient money (pp. 74–76) 7. Johnny: passion for beauty; Katie: soft ways (pp. 72–73) 8. become less important to Katie; She favors him over them (pp. 95–96). 9. great lover, great mother; loves and mothers everyone, including men (p. 100) 10. Sissy takes children on a bike ride without permission, lets them play with a container of condoms they open and display outside (pp. 117–121) **C.** Answers will vary. Refer to the scoring rubric on p. 46 of this guide.

Quiz #3: A. 1. d (p. 139) 2. h (pp. 145–146) 3. b (pp. 172–173) 4. f (pp. 154–158) 5. j (pp. 197, 211–213) 6. a (pp. 160–162) 7. i (p. 165) 8. g (pp. 182–183) 9. c (pp. 233–234) 10. e (pp. 128–129) **B.** Answers will vary. Refer to the scoring rubric on p. 46 of this guide.

Quiz #4: A. 1. F (pp. 256, 261) 2. F (pp. 269–271) 3. T (p. 281) 4. T (pp. 304–309) 5. F (p. 285) 6. T (pp. 350–351) **B.** Note: Answers to #7–#11 are on pp. 272–274, 279–287, and 321–324. 7. c 8. a 9. d 10. e 11. b **C.** Answers will vary. Refer to the scoring rubric on p. 46 of this guide.

Quiz #5: A. 1. Neeley (pp. 384–385) 2. a cup once strong but now cracked (pp. 386–387) 3. World War I (p. 401, implied) 4. she is afraid Katie won't let her go to high school (pp. 381–386) 5. tutoring her, checking her assignments, preparing her for finals (pp. 431–436) **B.** 6. get new bills and take the money to Katie (pp. 369–371) 7. was a test to see if Francie and Neeley have Johnny's tendency toward alcoholism (pp. 402–405) 8. goes to a hospital and doctor gives the baby oxygen (pp. 438–440) 9. asks her to promise to wait for him, then marries another girl the next day (pp. 454–463) 10. Katie agrees to marry McShane (pp. 469–471). **C.** Answers will vary. Refer to the scoring rubric on p. 46 of this guide.

Novel Test, Level One: A. 1. c 2. g 3. a 4. i 5. h 6. j 7. d 8. f 9. e 10. b **B.** 11. d (pp. 5–8, 135–138) 12. a (p. 6) 13. d (pp. 22–26) 14. b (p. 37) 15. d (p. 74) 16. d (p. 61) 17. b (p. 72) 18. a (pp. 98–99) 19. d (p. 109) 20. c (pp. 117–121) 21. b (pp. 139–140) 22. b (pp. 146–147) 23. d (pp. 153–157) 24. d (pp. 172–173) 25. a (pp. 197–199) 26. c (pp. 255, 261) 27. d (pp. 279–280) 28. c (p. 285) 29. b (pp. 304–309) 30. a (p. 323, implied) 31. b (p. 351) 32. b (pp. 368–370) 33. d (p. 303) 34. d (pp. 419–424) 35. c (pp. 438–439) 36. c (p. 463) 37. a (p. 471) 38. a (p. 477) 39. d (throughout) 40. c (implied) **C. & D.** Answers will vary. Refer to the scoring rubric on p. 46 of this guide.

Novel Test, Level Two: A. 1. imaginative, loyal, loving, intelligent, diligent; fear: attack of sexual predator; humiliation: doctor at clinic talks about her filth; compassion: women's mistreatment of Joanna; sorrow: Johnny's death 2. talented, weak, alcoholic; her favorite parent 3. pretty, resourceful, determined; provides stability and guidance 4. amusing, talented, reliable; her younger brother, confidant, companion 5. promiscuous, loving, kind, generous; her favorite aunt 6. meticulous, controlling; English teacher who disapproves of Francie's realistic writing 7. intelligent, handsome, helpful; her tutor and friend 8. manipulative, deceptive; causes her first heartbreak 9. loving, kind, determined; grandmother who inspires Francie's mother to get her a good education 10. generous, kind, faithful; provides money for college **B.** 11. a (pp. 34–35) 12. c (pp. 83–85) 13. a (p. 69) 14. b (pp. 79–80) 15. c (pp. 99–100) 16. d (pp. 149–150, 169–173, 351) 17. d (pp. 255–261) 18. a (pp. 304–305) 19. c (p. 471) 20. b (pp. 482–490) **C.** 21. Johnny; implicit comment on his own feeling of entrapment (p. 123) 22. Francie; Just as the cup is cracked, the family is developing cracks (p. 386). 23. Miss Garnder; insisting that Francie quit writing realistic stories about Johnny (p. 323) 24. Francie; Katie loves Neeley more but needs Francie during the birth process (p. 332). 25. Katie; her reaction to Francie's refusal to spend the night with Lee (p. 384) **D.** Responses will vary but should include the following information. 26. Francie's ability to grow and thrive in spite of adversity just as the Tree of Heaven does 27. Francie's escape from poverty and vicariously living in a better world 28. public opinion that she was bad because of her wild ways with men; has a good, generous heart 29. humiliation at the hands of a doctor and nurse, whom she should be able to trust 30. Katie's telling him of her pregnancy, stops drinking, stays out late and doesn't speak to the family, can't get work and is thrown out of Waiters' Union, collapses in street, dies without regaining consciousness **E.** Answers will vary. Refer to the scoring rubric on p. 46 of this guide.

Alternative Assessment: Answers will vary. Suggestions for #1–#4: 1. living conditions reflect pre-war poverty in Brooklyn, conversations in the saloon allude to people/places involved in the war, Francie loses her job as an indirect result of the war 2. growing up as a child selling junk for a few pennies, learning to frugally buy food, being spat upon by a child she trusts, starting school and experiencing the social "caste" system, surviving her experience with a sexual predator, losing her father, conflicting with Katie over high school, having to go to work to support the family, falling in love and having her heart broken, attaining her dream of college 3. person vs. person—Katie and Francie's conflict over school: resolved when Katie remains firm that Neeley will be the one to go and later when Francie attends college classes; person vs. society—the family's struggle against poverty: resolved when Francie gets a good job and eventually when Katie agrees to marry McShane; person vs. self—Johnny vs. his desire to drink: resolved when he dies 4. Johnny does not have much education (he had to go to work after sixth grade) and is forced to use his considerable talent in unsatisfying work as a singing waiter. Poverty created by family responsibilities means he never has the time or means to become a great singer or dancer. In addition, his alcoholism, which is aggravated by the stress of his responsibilities and impoverished circumstances, ensures him increasingly sporadic work and an early death. #5–#8: Answers will vary. Refer to the scoring rubric on p. 46 of this guide.

Linking Novel Units® Student Packets to National and State Reading Assessments

During the past several years, an increasing number of students have faced some form of state-mandated competency testing in reading. Many states now administer state-developed assessments to measure the skills and knowledge emphasized in their particular reading curriculum. This Novel Units® guide includes open-ended comprehension questions that correlate with state-mandated reading assessments. The rubric below provides important information for evaluating responses to open-ended comprehension questions. Teachers may also use scoring rubrics provided for their own state's competency test.

Scoring Rubric for Open-Ended Items

3-Exemplary
Thorough, complete ideas/information
Clear organization throughout
Logical reasoning/conclusions
Thorough understanding of reading task
Accurate, complete response

2-Sufficient
Many relevant ideas/pieces of information
Clear organization throughout most of response
Minor problems in logical reasoning/conclusions
General understanding of reading task
Generally accurate and complete response

1-Partially Sufficient
Minimally relevant ideas/information
Obvious gaps in organization
Obvious problems in logical reasoning/conclusions
Minimal understanding of reading task
Inaccuracies/incomplete response

0-Insufficient
Irrelevant ideas/information
No coherent organization
Major problems in logical reasoning/conclusions
Little or no understanding of reading task
Generally inaccurate/incomplete response

Notes

Notes